eat.shop denver

researched, photographed and written by
jan faust

cabazon books : 2008

table of contents

eat

shop

an's notes on denver

e travel brochures will tell you that denver fields teams for all four major sports, boasts a libeskind
ddition to its museum, is yodeling distance from the rockies, honors its wild west roots, and brews up
lot of mighty fine beers.

hat's harder to explain, but what i find to be denver's greatest feature, is the sense that the city is on
e cusp of "something big." maybe the modern equivalent of a gold rush, but one that values quality
ving more than riches. it's more a rush of energy, a rush of ideas. everywhere i went here, i felt the
appy confidence of denverites who know they're in the right place at the right time.

aybe it was the altitude-thinned air one whole mile in the sky, but i felt a lightheadedness bordering on
ddiness being in this place where the people know how to blend modern and historical, rural with city,
dependence with communal, and work with play. the end result is a cheerful populace, a beautiful city,
nd lots of exciting possibilities still to come.

eyond that general and pervasive sense of well-being, here are some specific things I found myself
ppreciating about denver:

> *diagonal crosswalks downtown*: why go left, then right, or vice versa, when you can simply cut
cross the street? brilliant.

> *architecturally-varied neighborhoods*: have a ball and drive around the cherry creek neighborhood,
any other 'hood, really, and see a federalist brick home, next to a rustic log cabin, next to a painted
dy victorian, next to a glass-fronted cube home. breathtaking!

> *the tattered cover*: some bookstores transcend. this is one of them—poll anyone. or just ask me or
y 5-year-old son; we were both besotted with the tattered cover. denver is lucky to have two of them.

> *insanely friendly people*: i mean that in the nicest possible way.

> *weather that keeps you guessing*: i like a surprise. i was surprised, for instance, when an 82-degree
ay was followed by a blizzard. extreme layering is, of course, the key. true denverites have it down and
ill be happy to share their expertise.

 have fun, layer up, don't be afraid to talk to the natives. and of course—eat, shop and enjoy!

arada

ethiopian specialties

750 santa fe drive. between seventh and eighth
303.329.3344 www.aradarestaurant.com
lunch tue - sat 11:30a - 2p dinner 5 - 10p sun 5 - 10p

opened in 1998. chef / owner: haime asfaw
$ - $$: all major credit cards accepted
lunch. dinner. full bar. first come, first served

santa fe arts district >

What is the key population density at which you get to have a great Ethiopian restaurant in your city? Whatever it is, Denver seems to have reached it because this city is graced with a number of fine Ethiopian restaurants. Among them, it's hard to do better than *Arada*, where Haime brings her traditional skills to the sublime combinations of berber-spiced meats and vegetable dishes, each somehow richer and more delicious than the next. And don't forget the tart injera bread—tear it, then use it to mop the goodness up. Denverites, you don't know how good you've got it.

imbibe / devour:
honey wine
doro wot
gored gored
bozena shiro
arada special hummus dip
kikil kitfo
tomato fit-fit
minchetabush

beatrice & woodsley

small plates. big wines.

38 south broadway. between ellsworth and archer
303.777.3505 www.beatriceandwoodsley.com
brunch sat - sun 10a - 3p tea & woodsley 3 - 5p
dinner daily 5p - 2a

opened in 2008. owners: kevin delk and john skogstad chef: pete list
$$ - $$$: all major credit cards accepted
brunch. afternoon tea. dinner. full bar. first come, first served

 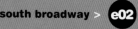

Generally, I don't cotton to dramatically designed restaurants. *Beatrice & Woodsley*, for all of its baroque Thomas Keller-goes-camping-aesthetic, is a rare and wonderful exception. Conceived in the fertile mind of Kevin Delk and primarily built with his own skilled hands, *B&W* is a wooded wonderland. Pete in the kitchen matches Kevin's design intensity with his turn-of-the-century comfort food. Every detail here has been considered, and every moment and every bite should be savored. Bring a sleeping bag—you'll probably want to camp out.

imbibe / devour:
kick in the eye cocktail
heidsieck monopole
turtle soup with cream sherry & whole egg
humble pie with veal & oysters
sweet pea cakes
angels on horseback
cod & cockles
crawfish beignets

biker jim's dogs

a hot-dog cart gone wild

corner of 16th and arapahoe. under the clock tower
www.bikerjimsdogs.com
concession mon - fri 6:30 - 9:30a
cart 11a - 4p

opened in 2005. chef / owner: jim pittenger
$: cash only
breakfast. lunch. coffee / tea. treats. first come, first served

central business district > 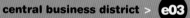**e03**

Biker Jim's low overhead is the big sky above. Stationed at his cart, on one corner of the pedestrian mall, Biker Jim is a one-man band turning out a delicious array of unusual and carefully sourced dogs, brats and sausages. Reindeer from Alaska and pheasant from neighboring states are exotic and popular, but you'll do fine even with a regular snappy frankfurter, sent over from the *Continental Deli*. If you have the misfortune of coming too early for Biker Jim, stop into the freakishly small concession stand steps away, tide yourself over with a coffee, and wait. It's worth it.

imbibe / devour:
elk jalapeño cheddar brat
pheasant sausage
louisiana red hot
glacier ice cream
cheesecake milk shake
kaladi brothers coffee
reindeer sausage breakfast burrito

bistro vendôme

a charming, romantic french restaurant

1420 larimer square. between 14th and 15th
303.852.3232 www.bistrovendôme.com
brunch sat - sun 10a - 2p
dinner mon - thu 5 - 10p fri - sat 5 - 11p sun 5 - 9p

opened in 2003. owners: beth gruitch and jennifer jasinski
executive chef: jennifer jasinski chef de cuisine: matt anderson
$$ - $$$: all major credit cards accepted
brunch. dinner. full bar. first come, first served

larimer square >

France is so darned far away. You have to take planes, shuttles, taxis. You get there, and the dollar's in a shamble, the people mock your French, and then there's a garbage strike. But you have one meal. One. In an amazing bistro tucked off a side street, with the sunlight slanting onto the mirrored menu wall, and you realize it was all worth it. That's the dream, but, obviously, not always possible. Go instead to *Bistro Vendôme*. Have a pernod aperitif. Tuck into the steak tartare. Enjoy the ambience. No it won't be France, but it will be *magnifique* and you'll go home without all that airport security hassle.

imbibe / devour:
05 marcel deiss, reisling
jacques cousteau cocktail
quiche aux truffes
crêpes vendôme
st. jacques poêlées
steak tartare
steak frites roquefort
blueberry lavender napoleon

bonnie brae ice cream

handmade ice cream in a retro setting

799 south university boulevard. corner of east ohio
303.777.0808 www.bonniebraeicecream.com
summer hours sun - thu 11a - 10p fri - sat 11a - 11p
winter hours sun - thu 11a - 8p fri - sat 11a - 9p

opened in 1986. owners: bob and cindy pailet and ken and judy simon
$: visa. mc
treats. first come, first served

old south gaylord >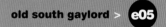

From the red and white striped awning to the slightly moldering giant mascot bear, *Bonnie Brae Ice Cream* radiates that old-time feeling. Even a few of the nice servers behind the counter are a bit long in the tooth. Fortunately, people knew a thing or two about this frozen concoction back in the day, so ice cream here doesn't have that "we're avant-garde, we'll try anything" feel but rather speaks to flavors perfected over time. Try the lemon custard—it demonstrates that with years, comes wisdom.

imbibe / devour:
seasonal housemade ice cream flavors:
  sinfully cinnamon
  triple death chocolate
  pumpkin pecan
  lemon custard
  red raspberry roll
blaster shake with toppings
special occasion cakes

13

brown palace hotel & spa

traditional afternoon tea at a denver institution

321 17th street. between broadway and tremont
303.297.3111 www.brownpalace.com
mon - sun noon - 4p

opened in 1892. executive chef: james gallo
$$: all major credit cards accepted
tea service. first come, first served

central business district > **e06**

When will people get honest and admit what they really like about afternoon tea? It's the petits fours, folks. It's the trimmed cucumber sandwiches. To call it a "multi-tiered, sweet and savory, silver-plated, snack-tray service" is probably too cumbersome when tea is so easy to say. For years I avoided afternoon tea until I realized what came with the tea. Here at the landmark *Brown Palace Hotel*, the high quality tea is well brewed and tasty. But the dainty macaroons and other sweet sustenances—all served with substance and style—those are exquisite.

imbibe / devour:
hot tea
cucumber tea sandwich
brown palace macaroons
centennial almond sponge cake
black cherry & pistachio mousse
chocolate-dipped strawberries
mango buttercream cookie
butterscotch & chocolate scones

continental deli

a european take on quality meats

250 steele street, suite 112. corner of third
303.388.3354 www.continentalsausage.com
tue - fri 9a - 5p sat 9a - 4p

opened in 1969. owners: jessica and eric gutknecht
$ - $$: mc. visa
breakfast. lunch. dinner. grocery. first come, first served

cherry creek north > 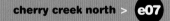 **e07**

While working on this book, I decided to test my will-power so I wouldn't have to go on a three-week, nut-and-berry diet post production. At *Continental Deli*, manager Renata handed me a warm frankfurter in a piece of waxed paper. Easy to dismiss, yes? Well, no. I snatched it up, popped it in and savored the brilliantly balanced saltiness, meatiness and snap of a perfectly produced frank. All bets were off from that day, and I cannot think of a better entry back to the delights of overconsumption. If the humble frank is that good here, it's no wonder they're considered "the best of the wurst."

imbibe / devour:
hungarian headcheese
bratwurst with sauerkraut
stuffed bacon with judgwurst
hofbauer noodle spaetzle
herring salad
goulash cream
dr. oetker black forest cake
gewurz ketchup

devil's food

a wonderful neighborhood café—not surly at all!
1024 south gaylord street. between tennessee and mississippi
303.733.7448 www.devilsfoodbakery.com
mon - fri 6a - 4p sat - sun 7a - 3p

opened in 1999. owner: angela patrick chef: juan herrerra
$ - $$: all major credit cards accepted
breakfast. lunch. coffee / tea. treats. wine / beer. first come, first served

old south gaylord >

It says so, right there on the business card, "open bright & surly." This is a refreshing acknowledgment that morning can be downright unpleasant until the body is properly stoked. Why not jump right into the fire, then, and start your day among others needing an attitude adjustment? The truth is, you will get it here at *Devil's Food*. You can't help but be cheered by the lovely space, the tempting menu, the loose-leaf tea and fresh coffee and the sinful desserts. If this be the devil's place, then I'm certainly going to h-e-double l.

imbibe / devour / covet:
dazbog coffee drinks
trout & eggs
apple brie sandwich
red velvet hedgehog
blood orange tarte
afternoon tea
frog & toad journals
welcome cookbooks

divino wine & spirits

a beautiful shop for finding top-drawer spirits

1240 south broadway. between arizona and louisiana
303. 778. 1800   www.divinowine.com
mon - thu 10a - 10p fri - sat 10a - 11p sun 10a - 6p

opened in 2003. owner: david moore
$$: all major credit cards accepted
liquor store. first come, first served

southwest > **e09**

Yes, I've used a wine bottle as a candle holder, but I've never thought of liquor bottles as art until I visited *Divino Wine & Spirits*. The selection of wines, grappas, tequilas, craft beers is impressive, but it's the way the bottles grace the walls that makes this spirits store stand apart. From the custom wooden shelving to the Saturday in-store tastings, *Divino* elevates the usual liquor shopping experience. The best thing though is the innovative silver tags which denote a bottle's price. Never again do you have to remove the smear of a sticker from your gift wine. So easy, so arty, so *Divino*.

imbibe / devour:
more than 100 grappas
02 andrake cellars cabernet franc
lurgashall english mead
jw lees harvest ale port cask
besserat de bellefon brut rosé
oud beersel framboise
j.k. scrumpy's hard cider
10 under 10 rack

domo japanese country foods

authentic, gorgeous and delicious japanese country restaurant

1365 osage street. between colfax and 13th
303.595.3666 www.domorestaurant.com
lunch mon - sat 11a - 2p
dinner 5 - 10p

opened in 1996. chef / owner: gaku homma
$$: mc. visa
lunch. dinner. wine / beer. reservations accepted for parties of six or more

central denver >

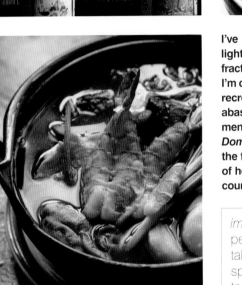

I've longed to go to Japan, specifically to the bright lights, big city of Tokyo. But if *Domo* conveys even a fraction of what it's like to visit the Japanese countryside, I'm changing my plans. So, do I think Gaku authentically recreates a countryside setting? Boy, do I. From his unabashed refusal to provide typical (and misused) condiments to the finest details of decor, everything about the *Domo* experience feels carefully curated. Then there's the food, with ritual side dishes and big-family servings of heartier fare all being precisely seasoned. Japanese countryside, here I come.

imbibe / devour:
persimmon leaf "kaki cha"
takara plum wine
spicy maguro donburi
teriyaki scallop shrimp & calamari
kaisoku nabe
wanko sushi
seafood curry
unagi toji

fruition

intimate restaurant with progressive, homegrown meals

1313 east sixth avenue. between marion and lafayette
303.831.1962 www.fruitionrestaurant.com
mon - sat 5 - 10p sun 5 - 8p

opened in 2007. owner: paul attardi chef / owner: alex seidel
$$ - $$$: all major credit cards accepted
dinner. reservations recommended

southeast > **e11**

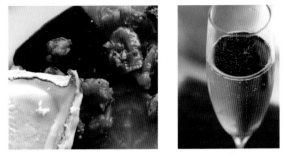

It took some time to coordinate with the owners of *Fruition*. It's small, they told me. We're busy, they reminded me. I was aware of both by reputation, but what I couldn't know firsthand until I got there was how beautifully their popular restaurant manages these conditions, so that you feel neither cramped nor rushed. If anything, you feel like you're in a warmly decorated home, except an expert staff and seasoned chef have just materialized with bags of super-fresh groceries. And a wine license. And skills. Yes, it took me a while to get here, but I'm glad I did.

imbibe / devour:
07 sineann pinot gris
laphroaig "quarter cask"
potato-wrapped oyster rockefeller
oven-roasted beet salad
pan-roasted walleye pike
colorado lamb strip loin
seared alaskan halibut cheeks
caramelized banana pudding

great divide brewing company

a taproom where the beer is supremely fresh

2201 arapahoe street. between 22nd and park avenue west
303.296.9460 ext 26 www.greatdivide.com
mon - fri 3 - 8p sat 2 - 7p

opened in 1994. founder / brewmaster: brian dunn
$ - $$: mc. visa
beer only. free tours and tastings. local food delivery. first come, first served

northwest >  **e12**

Although *Great Divide* is surely a reference to the nearby Continental Divide, it also no doubt speaks of the divide between the quantity vs. quality beer drinkers. You know—buy a beer because the 30-pack is on sale versus sip your session beer straight from the firkin. Lord knows, I have rappelled on both sides of this divide but am now firmly on the side of "fewer beers that taste great." Therefore, I was happy to trek over to the *Great Divide* taproom, to visit the beer where it's made, and taste it fresh from its kegs. It's a great way to spend an hour or two or six.

imbibe:
great divide company:
  samurai
  denver pale ale
  hercules double ipa
  hibernation ale
  hades
  yeti imperial stout
  old ruffian barley wine

happy cakes

because everyone deserves a little sugar

3815 west 32nd avenue. corner of newton
303.477.3556 www.happycakesdenver.com
tue - sat 10a - 6p

opened in 2007. owners: sara bencomo, lisa herman and laura reynolds
$: all major credit cards accepted
treats. first come, first served

highlands square > e13

We all know there are better ways to pair alcohol with dessert than jello shots. *Happy Cakes* may have found the perfect form. Inside their light, spongy cupcakes you might discover the happy tang of a cosmopolitan or the down-home jolt of Jack & Coke. Want to experiment? Show up during their all-day "happy hour" on Friday and see what barroom combos await. Kids will find cupcakes to their liking too, with traditional chocolates, vanillas and flavors changing daily and seasonally. No id required. *Happy Cakes* makes happy people, especially after eating a few cosmos.

imbibe / devour:
cupcakes:
  cosmo
  happy together
  peanut-butter cup
  chocolate stout
  mystery flavors on thursday
muttcakes for dogs
frosting shooters

il posto

the complicated simplicity of italian food and wine

2011 east 17th avenue. corner of race
303.394.0100 www.ilpostodenver.com
mon - thu 5:30 - 11p fri - sat 5:30 - midnight sun 5:30 - 10:30p

opened in 2007. chef / owner: andrea frizzi
$$ - $$$: all major credit cards accepted
dinner. full bar. reservations recommended

northeast >

There is no condiment as effective as fresh air, which is why I love to dine al fresco. If I'm dining this way, no matter where I am, I can envision myself with a companion savoring a perfect pasta-rich meal while sitting at a wrought-iron table in a fortressed medieval city. While *Il Posto* cannot exactly bring Italy to us, it can, with its patio and wide-open garage doors, offer us a wonderful outdoor dining experience with that inimitable spice of fresh air. Add Chef Andrea's dishes, inspired by his Milanese upbringing, and you are guaranteed both inner and outer happiness.

imbibe / devour:
alto adige d.o.c. pinot grigio
veneto rosso d.o.c. merlot
tagliere
doppio pesce
pappardelle salsiccia
capesante alla brace con verza all' aceto e pere
bistecca al cacao

kaladi coffee

coffee at its finest

1730 east evans avenue. between gilpin and williams
720.570.2166 www.kaladicoffee.com
mon - fri 6a - 7p sat 6:30a - 7p sun 7a - 5p

opened in 2000. owners: mark overly and andy melnick
$ - $$: all major credit cards accepted
coffee / tea. first come, first served

university park > 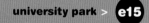 **e15**

Aha! Every *eat.shop guide* unearths at least one person who lives and breathes for the product that his or her business is based upon. Mark left his own coffee empire in Alaska when he could no longer personally guarantee each and every bean. Now at *Kaladi Coffee*, he sees a cup through the whole cycle, from selecting the beans, to roasting, grinding, pulling and pouring. He's had specialized equipment designed to his specs so he can produce "the reference" sample by which he judges each batch. Put yourself in Mark's hands and see how good coffee can be. You too can taste his passion.

imbibe / devour:
roasted on site coffee:
   dominican republic barahona
   sumatra aceh gayo mountain
   estate java jampi
   trieste caffe espresso
chemex 10 cup coffee maker
espresso made with puravidda café
xocolatl mocha

lola

a lively spot for fresh, coastal mexican flavors

1575 boulder street. corner of 16th
720.570.8686 www.loladenver.com
brunch sat - sun 10a - 2p
dinner mon - thu 4 - 10p fri 4 - 11p sat 5 - 11p sun 5 - 9p

opened in 2002. owner: big red f executive chef: jamey fader
$$: all major credit cards accepted
brunch. dinner. full bar. first come, first served

lohi >

When people call alcohol 'spirits,' they ain't kiddin'. And nothing is more possessed by infernal shades than tequila. At *Lola,* that means more than 100 mischievous spooks await you with their unparalleled range of tequila and, therefore, an equal number of ways to misbehave. So, how do you keep the tequila from going all Linda Blair on you? You eat, friends. You absorb the fresh, tableside guacamole. You coat your insides with the protective power of poblano tamales. That way, when the devil in the tequila strikes, not only will you be ready, but you will have had a great meal.

imbibe / devour:
100 kinds of tequila
lolarita
avocado fondue
tableside guacamole
lobster posole
banana-crusted snapper
mexican pot roast
roasted pineapple cajeta cake

m & d's bar-b-que & fish palace

down-home cooking in a family-run restaurant
2000 east 28th avenue. corner of race
303.296.1760
tue - thu 11a - 8p fri 11a - 10p sat 2 - 10p sun noon - 6p

opened in 1977. owners: mack and daisy shead
$ - $$: all major credit cards accepted
lunch. dinner. wine / beer. first come, first served

northeast > **e17**

Has this ever happened to you? Have you ever woken with the biological imperative to devour sauce-smothered, slow-cooked ribs? I have, and when I do, toast is an insult, omelets are weak, and hash browns are criminal. That's when I hike myself over to *M & D's*. I might have to kill a few hours because they don't open until 11am. Perhaps those hours could be spent working myself into a rib frenzy, to be richly rewarded when the hot, vibrantly red ribs are placed in front of me. A girl has needs, and *M & D's* knows how to meet them.

imbibe / devour:
fanta strawberry
fried green tomatoes
ribs, ribs, ribs
homemade hotlinks
mo betta burger
peppa fries
banana puddin'
lemon-glazed poundcake

marczyk fine foods

your world-class neighborhood market

770 east 17th avenue. corner of clarkson
303.894.9499 www.marczykfinefoods.com
mon - sat 8a - 8p sun 10a - 8p

opened in 2002. owners: pete and paul marczyk and barbara macfarlane
$ - $$: all major credit cards accepted
grocery. beer / wine. first come, first served

uptown >

Full disclosure: Pete and Paul, the men behind *Marczyk Fine Foods* are Red Sox fans. I'm a Red Sox fan. What they're doing in Denver and how they survived the 2007 World Series that pitted their favorite team against the Rockies is irrelevant here. What matters is that *Marczyk* provides a local alternative to the big grocery store experience. A good percentage of the shelves here are devoted to products made in and around Denver, which is a great way to show hometown pride. And their deli, featuring Niman Ranch meats, makes some killer sandwiches. Naturally, I recommend "The Fenway."

imbibe / devour:
the fenway sandwich
the chevrelet sandwich
pork green chili stew
niman ranch meats
spinelli's pasta sauce
elaine greens
munsun farms corn & squash
great wine selection

neighborhood flix cinema & café

feeding the urban appetite for food and film

2510 east colfax avenue. corner of columbine
303.777.3549 www.flixonthefax.com
mon - sun 11a - 10p (kitchen closes)

opened in 2007. owners: jimmie smith, melodie gaul and michelle dorant
$ - $$: all major credit cards accepted
brunch. lunch. dinner. full bar. first come, first served

city park >

Dinner and a movie should be like Bogie & Bacall. Like Astaire & Rogers. Why then, is it so often like Carrot Top & Pia Zadora? You spend $20 on the tickets and then another $30 on grease-laden popcorn and diluted soda. At *Neighborhood Flix*, it's all class all the way. Savory, addictive sweet-potato fries or smoked-salmon dip make for easy finger food when the lights go down. Luxe leather seats cradle you in style. The theater is clean and high tech, and the movies are of good quality. *Neighborhood Flix* is like Redford & Newman together again.

imbibe / devour:
basil grapefruit martini
leopolda blackberry rickey
buffalo meatloaf
vietnamese egg rolls
sweet potato fries
cheese board
smoked salmon dip
bottomless tub of popcorn

osteria marco

casual, quality italian fare

1453 larimer street. between 14th and 15th
303.534.5855 www.osteriamarco.com
mon - thu 11a - 10p fri 11a - 11p sat noon - 11p sun noon - 10p

opened in 2007. owners: frank bonanno, jean-philippe failyau and ryan gaudin
chef: jean-philippe failyau   sommelier: ryan gaudin
$$: all major credit cards accepted
lunch. dinner. full bar. first come, first served

larimer square > 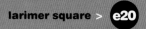 **e20**

Somewhere in the recent past, parmesan became parmigiano, and pasta tasted better. Then salami became salumi, and antipasti miraculously improved. Now osterias have joined pizzerias in our collective vernacular, and Italian dining has found its groove. Finding the balance that allows for thoughtful delicious foods in an unfussy atmosphere is welcome in any setting. Situated on busy Larimer Square, the downstairs *Osteria Marco* makes the perfect retreat from the bustle above. Don't skip the gnocco fritto.

imbibe / devour:
04 barbaresco, produttori del barbaresco
meat & potatoes cocktail
salumi plate
gnocco fritto
pancetta, burrata, lettuce & tomato sandwich
wild mushroom & robiola pizza
sunday night slow-roasted suckling pig
oven-baked fondata

pajama baking company

modern, indoor / outdoor market with homemade goods

1595 south pearl street. corner of iowa
303.733.3622   www.pajamabakingcompany.com
mon - sun 7a - 10p

opened in 2008. owners: the hutcheson and meyer families
$$: all major credit cards accepted
bakery. grocery. treats. first come, first served

old south pearl >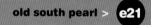

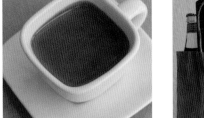

Baking and pajamas are both really excellent things. I can barely think of two better words to pair. Maybe brie & puppies? Or world peace & tiramisu? The folks at *Pajama Baking Company* have done well though, invoking not only the idea of oven-baked delights, but also the comfortable apparel in which to enjoy them. Don't show up in your pajamas though, (you probably could—I'm just looking out for you.) but do show up. Whether you come for the prepared foods and gourmet grocery items, the locally roasted coffee, or yes, the baked goods, this is food worth getting dressed for.

imbibe / devour:
coda coffee
cherry vanilla malt
pecan tarts
apple galette
brioche
freshly baked bread!
housemade sorbets & ice cream
gourmet market foods

45

same café

wonderfully different donation-based meals

2023 east colfax avenue. between race and vine
720.530.6853 www.soallmayeat.org
tue - fri 11a - 2p sat 11a - 8p

opened in 2006. owners: brad and libby birky
$: all major credit cards accepted
lunch. dinner. first come, first served

northeast >

It doesn't come right out and say it, but the 'same' in *Same Café* stands for, "so all may eat," which reveals the mission of this donation-based restaurant. It might more accurately have been named *Samew*, which would allow the word *well* to be appended to the name. But this doesn't sound as good, nor does it match up with the tagline, "wonderfully different" which is what the organic and healthy fare here is. So come in, enjoy a pear and gorgonzola pizza, drop the amount you're comfortable giving in the donation box or, alternatively, volunteer in the kitchen. It's all the same to them, and it's all good.

imbibe / devour:
oogavé soda
spinach & strawberry salad
pear & gorgonzola pizza
black bean soup
blt pasta salad
lentil apple salad
sugar cookies

savory spice shop

small-batch seasonings and spices

1537 platte street. between 15th and 17th
303.477.3322 www.savoryspiceshop.com
mon - fri 10a - 6p sat 10a - 5p sun 11a - 4p
see website for second location

opened in 2004. owners: mike and janet johnston
$ - $$: all major credit cards accepted
first come, first served

lohi >

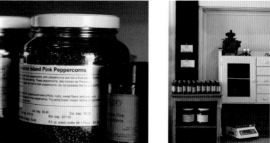

If they charged admission here at the *Savory Spice Shop*, I wouldn't mind at all. I'd stand in line, pay the ticket price (whatever the cost), get my day pass and emerge hours later, feeling thoroughly satisfied. In my time spent in this spare and rustic store, I would have, simply by smell, traveled the exotic spice routes, visited the capitals of barbeque country, and recalled favorite pie-making memories. With minimal packaging and maximum variety, *Savory Spice Shop* is the ultimate theme park for spice lovers.

imbibe / devour:
lodo red adobo
pumpkin seed oil
dried mushrooms
team sweet mama's kansas city rub
variety of fleur de sels
mortars & pestles
salt & pepper grinders
kuhn rikon spice grinder

senor burritos

good ol' hearty mexican meals

12 east first avenue. corner of broadway
second location in lakewood
303.733.0747
mon - sat 8a - 9p

opened in 1990. owners: the baylon family
$ - $$: all major credit cards accepted
lunch. dinner. first come, first served

south broadway > 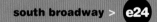 **e24**

The day I ate at *Senor Burritos*, I hadn't made any advance plans. I just showed up. Then I did as any good researcher does and ordered the deluxe green-chili smothered pork burrito, the menudo, a fish taco and flan. The menu taker's eyes got as wide as tortillas when I said I was alone. All in a day's work, right? So far, so normal, except for the part where I then completely hoovered the meal. I impressed even myself. Admittedly, I had to take the flan in the car with me, but you better believe I ate it. Everything is outstanding here—next time I'm going to eat the other half of the menu.

imbibe / devour:
jarritos
huevos ala mexicana
adobada burrito
green-chili-smothered desebrada burrito
soft pork chop tacos
fish tacos
texas toothpicks
sopapilla

snooze

an a.m. eatery (and drinkery)
2262 larimer street. corner of 23rd
303.297.0700 www.snoozedenver.com
mon - fri 6:30a - 2:30p sat - sun 7a - 2:30p

opened in 2006. owners: jon and adam schlegel   chef: brenda buenviaje
$$: all major credit cards accepted
breakfast. lunch. full bar. first come, first served

northwest >

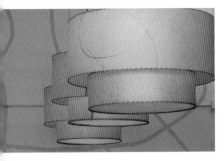

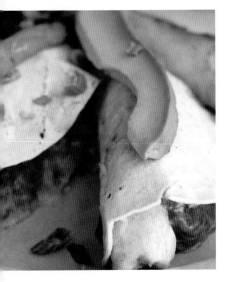

I'm not sure a "right to choose" is something that I am a big fan of. I consider it a chore to choose. A burden, even. Because I'm not very good at choosing. I want this and I want that. I prefer the "right to have both." Or better, the "right to have all three." At *Snooze*, you can do that, with a flight of pancakes, three flavors, so you don't have to choose. And I appreciate this for the days when I'm craving sweet. But most days I wake up wanting savory. If they could just do the breakfast tacos and pancake flight, I wouldn't even have to make that choice.

imbibe / devour:
mimosa
granola split
pineapple-upside-down pancakes
good ol' biscuits & gravy
gimme gimme pillow toast
pancake flight
sloppy josephina
bison meatball sub

sputnik

street foods under one rambunctious roof

3 south broadway. corner of ellsworth
720.570.4503 www.sputnikdenver.com
mon - sun 10:30a - 2a

opened in 2003. owners: allison and matt labarge chef: matthew parris
$ - $$: all major credit cards accepted
weekend breakfast. lunch. dinner. full bar. first come, first served

south broadway > 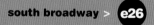 e26

How many times have we heard continent-tripping gourmands talk about their Michelin restaurant experience but then smugly note that the "chile-laced arepa from one of the local street carts was the most memorable meal of the trip." Operating on the almost universal allure of street food, particularly among the young explorer types, *Sputnik* delivers a variety of straightforward, unpretentious but delicious offerings spanning the globe. Not feeling adventurous? There's always corn dogs and cold PBRs. Hard to top.

imbibe / devour:
caffé vita coffee
mojitos with homemade coconut-infused vodka
mango bread french toast
corn dog
sweet potato fries
cuban pork sandwich
cold jicama salad
funnel cakes

st. mark's coffee house

more than a coffee house, a social hub

2019 east 17th street. corner of race
303.322.8384 www.stmarkscoffeehouse.com
mon - thu 7a - midnight fri - sat 7a -11:30p sun 7a - 10:30p

opened in 1993. owner: eric alsted
$ - $$: all major credit cards accepted
breakfast. lunch. dinner. coffee / tea. first come, first served

northeast > e27

I am a somewhat peripatetic writer. I'll start in one place, hit a wall. Go to the next place. Hit a wall. Eventually though, I reach a point where the wandering has to stop, and I choose a place to get busy. *St. Mark's* creates the perfect environment for settling in. Its big garage doors provide plenty of natural light, the coffee is stiff and motivating, you can sit inside in the front or move to the shaded back when you want to retreat from the madding crowd. And then there are nice carb-laden foods to nourish you. As noted, there are many reasons for loving this Denver institution.

imbibe / devour:
espresso roma java
30+ loose leaf teas
great cookies
chocolate cheese cake
raspberry tart
gorgonzola & spinach panini

steuben's

a modern update on the classic american diner

523 east 17th avenue. corner of pearl
303.830.1001 www.steubens.com
mon - thu 11a - 11p fri 11a - midnight sat 10a - midnight sun 10a - 11p

opened in 2006. owner: josh wolkon owner and executive chef: matt selby
chef: brandon biederman
$$: all major credit cards accepted
brunch. lunch. dinner. full bar. first come, first served

uptown >

You could almost imagine *Steuben's* as a chain, in the *Johnny Rockets* vein, celebrating nostalgic American foods and the diner aesthetic. Fortunately, *Steuben's* is not a chain, so when you pop in for the lobster roll, you'll get generous heapings of fresh, sweet, chunky meat stashed between bulky rolls. And unlike a chain, here you'll find servers with character and a cadre of regulars who have made *Steuben's* their place to meet for after-work drinks. These are the hallmarks of a fine casual restaurant with a plan, and fortunately not one of global domination.

imbibe / devour:
moscow mule
shrimp 'n' grits
habanero honey-fried corn
deviled eggs
maine lobster roll & fries
cayenne étouffée
truck stop chocolate cake
butterscotch pudding

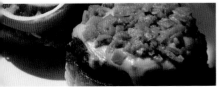

sushi sasa

the intersection of traditional and progressive japanese delicacies

2401 15th street, suite 80. corner of platte
303.433.7272 www.sushisasadenver.com
mon - sat 11:30a - 2:30p sun - thu 5 - 10:30p fri - sat 5 - 11:30p

opened in 2005. owner / chef: wayne conwell
$$ - $$$: all major credit cards accepted
lunch. dinner. reservations recommended

lohi >

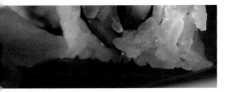

The quiet palette of blond woods and variations on white are the yin of the *Sushi Sasa* equation. The yang—the colorful, chromatic, spectacular yang—is the taste of the sushi and the other dishes here. Fresh ingredients are shipped in daily from the fish markets of Japan, to be fashioned by chef/owner Wayne and his staff into confident spins on traditional master recipes. Each precise delicacy bursts into flavor, like a rainbow of the sea. Order the omakase, the Chef's Choice, and let Wayne reveal that there are colors you didn't even know existed.

imbibe / devour:
premium imported sakes
chawan musi
warm octopus carpaccio salad
scallop tomato fondue
tara saikyo yuan
anago kampyo roll
big-o tempura roll

table 6

a sweet and spunky restaurant
609 corona street. corner of 6th
303.831.8800 www.table6denver.com
mon - sun 5 - 11p sun 10:30a - 2p, 5 - 8:30p

opened in 2004. owners: aaron forman and dan ferguson chef: scott parker
$$ - $$$: all major credit cards accepted
brunch. dinner. wine / beer. first come, first served

southwest >

I think one of the defining conditions of being a neighborhood restaurant is to be open seven days a week. Any number of scenarios, at any time, can make you need to take refuge in a comfortable, friendly environment. Your hungry friend drops in unannounced. You realize you're completely out of olive oil. Your kids are getting on your last nerve. Any one of those could be all it takes to cause you to surrender and say, "That's it! We're going out!" Wonderful, then, to have a place like *Table 6*, a laid-back but food-serious place open daily. Have a glass of the wacky scrumptious wine of the night and relax.

imbibe / devour:
wacky scrumptious wine of the night
breakfast charcuterie
crumpets, tasso ham & hollandaise
baked granola, greek yogurt & fruit
grilled prawns, grits & spinach
malt-baked black cod
pineapple upside-down pig
lamb reuben sliders

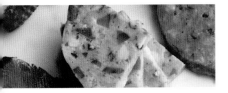

tacos y salsas #3

a casual mexican restaurant with mexican classics

910 south federal boulevard. corner of kentucky
303.922.9400
sun - thu 8a - 10p fri - sat 8a - 2a

$: all major credit cards accepted
breafast. lunch. dinner. full bar. first come, first served

southwest >

I just wasn't thinking. I planned my visit to *Tacos y Salsas* on the 5th of May. With my "I'm a Gringo" lapel button. Well, no, I don't have one of those, but you'd think I'd remember Cinco de Mayo. South Federal Boulevard was cordoned off with barriers at every cross street and with policemen at every turn to limit the semi-spontaneous parades the street is known for on the holiday. So, I parked a mile or so away and hoofed it. I threaded through big groups to get my taco fix. How *alegre* I was about my meal here and all its fixin's. You must visit soon—just maybe not on May 5th.

imbibe / devour:
horchata
huevos con chorizo
adobada burrito
al pastor gorditas
chicken flautas
deshebrada street acos
coctel de camron

the british bulldog

get your peshawari and bitter ale fix here

2052 stout street. corner of broadway
303.295.7974 www.britishbulldogdenver.com
mon - fri 11a - 2a sat - sun 7a - 2a

opened in 2006. owner: isaac james chef: thomas cortez
$ - $$: all major credit cards accepted
breakfast. lunch. dinner. full bar. first come, first served

northwest >  **e32**

The *eat.shop* research process is a complicated one, but it often yields fun finds. My friend Josh, a graphic designer in Providence, has a friend, John, who runs a competitive trivia contest in bars in Denver called "Geeks who Drink." I call John to feel him out for places he likes, and he tells me that he's going to *The British Bulldog*. You mean, the futball-loving, fish & chip serving, 1930s mural-painted bar that also serves Pakistani specialties? How could I not go to such a place? Believe me, it became an immediate fave for me, and it will for you too.

imbibe / devour:
fullers london pride draught
english breakfast with rashers, bangers &
   blood pudding
french toast bombay style
pub balls
anglo indian meatballs
chappli kebabs
peshawari chicken salad

the cherry cricket

the black sheep of cherry creek

2641 east second avenue. corner of clayton
303.322.7666 www.cherrycricket.com
mon - sun 11a - midnight bar 11a - 2a

opened in 1990
$ - $$: all major credit cards accepted
lunch. dinner. full bar. first come, first served

cherry creek north > **e33**

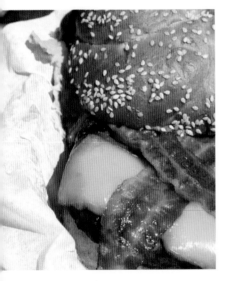

The door at *The Cherry Cricket* never stays shut for long. It's yanked open in a seemingly endless drumbeat of people taking refuge from the tony streets of Cherry Creek for the comforting dive-y-ness here. As far as I could tell, people kept coming in, and the restaurant kept getting more and more packed. Nor did I ever see anybody leave. For all I know, they're still there now, enjoying smothered green-chile fries or the popular Cricket burger. Or playing a game of pool, or sitting on the patio. You can be sure that even as I write, more are still coming in.

imbibe / devour:
odell brewing "90 shilling ale"
cricket burger
chili con queso
mac & cheese wedges
messy bean nachos
turkey reuben
smothered green-chili cheese fries
herbed artichoke dip

the cruise room

1930s glamour frozen in time
1600 17th street. corner of wazee
303.825.1107 www.theoxfordhotel.com
mon - sun 4:30 - 11:45p

opened in 1933. managed by mccormick's fish house & bar
$$: all major credit cards accepted
dinner. full bar. first come, first served

lodo > **e34**

We are, every one of us, seductive and alluring at *The Cruise Room*. I know, because I was hit on here. In the dark space, with the light coming from the red-neon fixtures, illuminating the 1930s era friezes, and bouncing off the original chrome, you are taken back to a time of glamour, stiff drinks and the dawn of international travel. The design here is modeled after one of the lounges on The Queen Mary, and after a lemon drop or three, you might actually think you feel the room rocking along on waves. Plan your trip to *The Cruise Room* now and be ready for exotic ports of call.

imbibe:
lemon drop
pink flamingo
golden goose
fresca
perfect martini
white cosmopolitan
peachy keen

the shoppe

cereal, cupcakes and design goods

3103 east colfax avenue. between steele and saint paul
303.322.3969 www.theshoppedenver.com
tue - thu 11a - 10p fri - sat 11a - 2a

opened in 2008. owners: emma skala and tran wills
$: all major credit cards accepted
coffee / tea. treats. first come, first served

city park > **e35**

Let the giant bricks of butter be your guide as to whether *The Shoppe* serves good cupcakes. Perhaps when you visit, the dozen or so pounds of butter are out of sight. Then let the smell inform you. I found this place dizzy-making, in the best possible way, from the hot-pink walls to the intense aroma of cream-cheese frosting that perfumes the air. In addition to offering transcendent cupcakes and scads of breakfast cereals, *The Shoppe* also fashions itself as a community space for both movie screenings and cake decorating seminars. But anyway, back to the cupcakes.

imbibe / devour/ covet:
cupcakes:
  .oreo
  strawberry champagne
  pineapple tastiness
cold-cereal combos with toppings
hyland mather cupcake art
cupcake books & paraphernalia
dee projects pot holders

the tea box

tea and dim sum served daily
2353 east third avenue. corner of university
303.393.7972
mon - thu 9:30a - 7p fri 9:30a - 6p sat 9:30a - 7p sun 11a - 6p

opened in 2004. owner: regina chan
$ - $$: mc. visa
lunch. dinner. coffee / tea. first come, first served

cherry creek north > **e36**

I'm an occasional tea drinker, but I'm always trying to expand my interest in and exposure to it. Therefore I wanted to check out *The Tea Box*. Here on offer are estate-quality, whole leaf teas and gyokuro teas which are both important to tea aficiandos. And while I appreciated these teas and the other rare ones available, it was the presentation of the dim sum tray that wowed me. I may never be a big tea drinker, but I'm a big eater, and this collection of precious, nearly translucent, tiny delicacies will ensure my return to *The Tea Box*.

imbibe / devour:
gyokuro teas
green snow needle tea
green tea roll
lemon & apple tarts
dim sum plate
asian pear salad
peanut butter apple sandwich
hummus & turkey sandwich

the thin man

narrow bar with wide reputation

2015 east 17th avenue. between race and vine
303.320.7817 www.thinmantavern.com
sun - thu 4p - 2a fri - sat 3p - 2a

opened in 1993. owner: eric alsted
$: all major credit cards accepted
dinner. full bar. first come, first served

northeast > e37

I've always wanted to be Nora Charles so I could drink all day with my besotted husband by my side and my little terrier at my heels—to solve murder mysteries for fun, to be an heiress! This is sadly not my life, except that while I work I can drink all day... okay, maybe just for several hours in the evening. And when I do, *The Thin Man's* the place to do it. Channeling Nora, I would select one of the fruit-infused vodkas as my drink of choice. I'd craft some arch comment about all the Jesus memorabilia on the wall. I'd lounge against the bar and wait for my Nick to come, drink in hand, witty repost at the ready.

imbibe / devour:
housemade fruit & herb infused vodkas
single malts
abita amber beer
man beer english ipa
turkey jalapeño panini
homemade soup with bread
bowl of olives

the truffle cheese shop

artisan cheeses and exotic foods

2906 east sixth avenue. between milwaukee and fillmore
303.322.7363 www.denvertruffle.com
mon - sat 10a - 6p sun 10a - 4p

opened in 2001. owners: robert and karin lawler
$ - $$: all major credit cards accepted
grocery. lunch. first come, first served

cherry creek north >

When I lived in New York, I developed a robust passion for sausages and cured meats made in the Italian style. My husband and I were fans of *Faicco Bros.*, then we got turned on to the row of meat markets on the Bronx's Arthur Avenue. So when *The Truffle Cheese Shop's* owner Rob handed me a heavenly slice of Bresaola, I nearly dismissed it. Mistake! Turned out, it was from the legendary *Salumeria Biellese*. I should have known. *Truffle* sources from the best places, far and near, including local farmstead cheeses—so you cannot go wrong here, and you might even learn a thing or two.

imbibe / devour:
fresh truffles & truffle products
breadworks fresh breads
haystack mt. goat cheese
james ranch cheese
amarena cherries from italy
minnie beasley's almond lace cookies

watercourse foods

eat the path of least resistance

837 east 17th avenue. between emerson and clarkson
303.832.7313 www.watercoursefoods.com
mon - fri 7a - 10p sat - sun 8a - 10p

opened in 2007. owner: dan landis chef: matt dwyer
$$: all major credit cards accepted
breakfast. lunch. dinner. treats. wine / beer. first come, first served

uptown >

I have full admiration for vegetarians and even greater respect for vegans. I have tried (and have failed) to cut out meat at several points in my long and winding life (note my ode to sausage on the previous page). And while my respect hasn't waned because of this, it seems to me that it's a heckuva lot easier to be a vegetarian or vegan these days on account of the amazing dishes that places like *Watercourse* are pioneering. Everything coming out of this kitchen here is appealing, natural and delicious. So maybe I'll never be a vegetarian, but I can certainly be a dedicated lover of *Watercourse*.

imbibe / devour:
vegan milk shake
juju ginger ale on tap
sweet potato cinnamon roll
banana bread french toast
blackened tofu
dona lee sandwich
frings (half french fries, half onion rings)
build your own salad

wazee supper club

the granddaddy of lodo
1600 15th street. corner of wazee
303.623.9518 www.wazeesupperclub.com
mon - sat 11a - 2a sun noon - midnight

opened in 1974. chef: randy belch
$ - $$: all major credit cards accepted
lunch. dinner. full bar. reservations recommended

lodo > **e40**

The Wazee Supper Club has been around for almost 40 years, a long hitch by any measure, but it feels like its heyday might have been 70 or 80 years ago. A black and white parquet floor, a once-purloined telegraph clock, stained-glass windows of dubious origin, and benches from a shuttered Elks Club give this "Granddaddy of Lodo" its prohibition-era feel. For all of its historic trappings, *Wazee* is still spunky and always packed, producing endless amounts of grub. Is it possible that all these natives and tourists are really just turning out for the celebrated dumbwaiter ? I don't think so.

imbibe / devour:
wynkoop rail yard ale
blackened salmon salad
wazee wings
bianca-style pizza
blue-steak sandwich
portobello melt
build your own stromboli

wen chocolates

unrivaled, small-batch, artisan chocolates
1541 platte street. between 15th and 17th
303.477.5765 www.wenchocolates.com
tue - fri 10a - 6p sat 10a - 5p sun 11a - 4p

opened in 2003. owners: loren penton and will poole
$ - $$: all major credit cards accepted
treats. first come, first served

lohi > **e41**

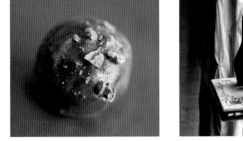

Earlier in this book, I celebrated a coffee purveyor for his passion, stating that you typically find just one beyond-the-pale passionate owner in each town. Denver, you've got two! No, three! The gentlemen at *Wen Chocolates* are off the charts with their dedication and skill at producing sublime chocolates. Their truffles are beautifully crafted with lovely dustings and sugared hints of what lies inside. No wacky shapes or printed patterns, just orbs of nuanced and decadent flavors, one taste of which could make a choir of angels—or me, for that matter—sing.

imbibe / devour:
chocolates truffles:
  mojca
  savannah
  kaffir lime
  pain d'epices
  violette
apple crostini
artisan chili bread

about

- all of the businesses featured in this book are locally owned. in deciding the businesses to featu we require this first and foremost. and then we look for businesses that strike us as utterly authent whether they be new or old, chic or funky. and since this is not an advertorial guide, businesses do r pay to be featured.

- explore from neighborhood to neighborhood. note that almost every neighborhood featured has doze of great stores and restaurants other than our favorites listed in this book.

- the maps in this guide are not highly detailed but instead are representational of each area noted. highly suggest, if you are visiting, to also have a more detailed map. streetwise maps are always a go bet, and are easy to fold up and take along with you.

- make sure to double check the hours of the business before you go by calling or visiting its websi often the businesses change their hours seasonally. also, businesses that are featured sometimes clos this is often the sobering reality for many small, local businesses.

- the pictures and descriptions of each business are representational. please don't be distraught wh the business no longer carries or is not serving something you saw or read about in the guide.

- the *eat.shop* clan consists of a small crew of creative types who travel extensively and have dedicat themselves to great eating and interesting shopping around the world. each of these people writes, ph tographs and researches his or her own books, and though they sometimes do not live in the city of t book they author, they draw from a vast network of local sources to deepen the well of information us to create the guides.

- there are three ranges of prices noted for restaurants, $ = cheap, $$ = medium, $$$ = expensive

eat.shop.sleep

here are many great places to stay in denver, but here are a few of my picks:

the oxford hotel (lodo)
1600 17th street
303.628.5400 / theoxfordhotel.com
standard double from $220
restaurant: mccormick's fish house & bar
bar: the cruise room
notes: consummately gracious, beautifully appointed and friendly

the curtis hotel
1405 curtis street (central business district)
303.571.0300 / thecurtis.com
standard double from $209
restaurant: the corner office
notes: wacky fun with themed floors.

hotel teatro
1100 14th street (central business district)
303.228.1100 / hotelteatro.com
standard double from $239
restaurant: restaurant kevin taylor
notes: luxury boutique hotel across from the denver center for the performing arts

the brown palace hotel & spa
321 17th street (central business district)
303.297.3111 / brownpalace.com
standard double from $270
restaurants & bar: see website
notes: storied, historic and elegant. host to presidents and luminaries for more than a century.

holiday chalet
1820 e. colfax (northeast)
303.437.8245 / holidaychalet.net
standard double from $120
notes: restored victorian b & b outside of downtown offers homey touches and charming quirks.

- highlands
- highlands square

eat

e13 > happy cakes

shop

s7 > dragonfly
s14 > max & me
s16 > mike's toys and hobbies
s28 > rejuvanest
s31 > strut
s32 > studio bead
s43 > wordshop

note: all maps face no

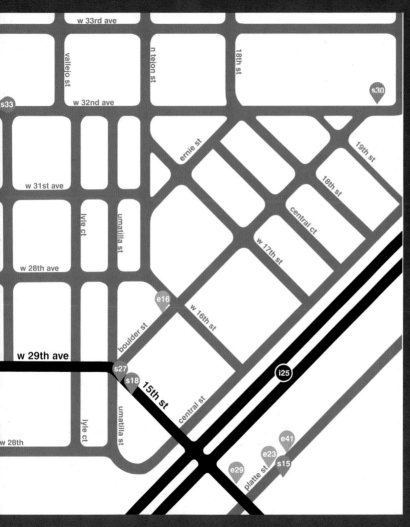

highlands •
lo-hi •

eat

e16 > lola
e23 > savory spice shop
e29 > sushi sasa
e41 > wen chocolates

shop

s15 > metroboom
s18 > mona lucero
s27 > red door swingin'
s30 > sportique scooters
s33 > swank

note: all maps face north

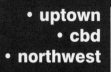

- **uptown**
- **cbd**
- **northwest**

eat

e3 > biker jim's dogs
e6 > brown palace
hotel & spa
e12 > great divide brewery
e18 > marczyk fine foods
e25 > snooze
e28 > steuben's
e32 > the british bulldog
e39 > watercourse

shop

s34 > talulah jones

lo-do•
larimer •
square

eat

e4 > bistro vendôme
e10 > domo
e20 > osteria marco
e34 > the cruise room
e40 > wazee supper club

shop

s5 > composition
s6 > cry baby ranch
s29 > rockmount ranch wear
s42 > urban lifestyle

note: all maps face north

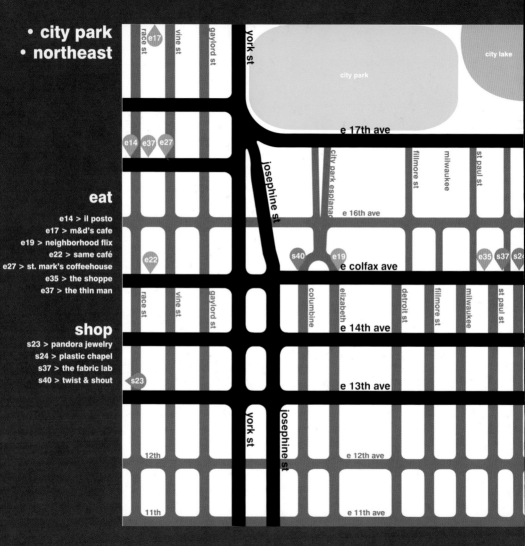

- **city park**
- **northeast**

eat

e14 > il posto
e17 > m&d's cafe
e19 > neighborhood flix
e22 > same café
e27 > st. mark's coffeehouse
e35 > the shoppe
e37 > the thin man

shop

s23 > pandora jewelry
s24 > plastic chapel
s37 > the fabric lab
s40 > twist & shout

note: all maps face no

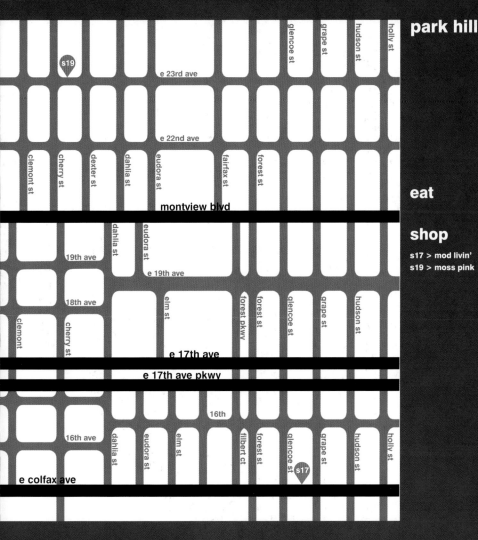

park hill

eat

shop

s17 > mod livin'
s19 > moss pink

note: all maps face north

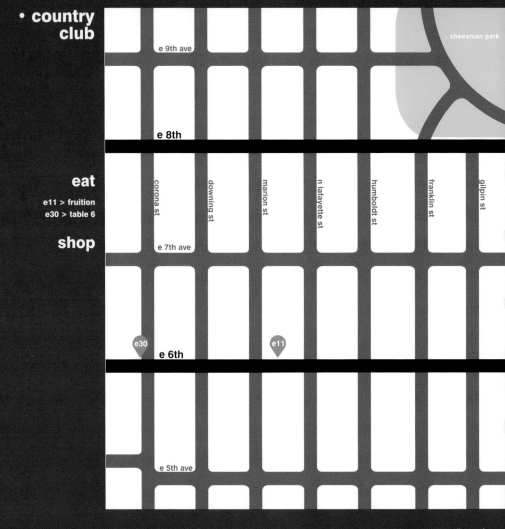

- **country club**

eat

e11 > fruition
e30 > table 6

shop

cheesman park

e 9th ave

e 8th

corona st

downing st

marion st

n lafayette st

humboldt st

franklin st

gilpin st

e 7th ave

e30

e11

e 6th

e 5th ave

cherry creek north

eat

e7 > continental deli
e33 > the cherry cricket
e36 > the tea box
e38 > the truffle
cheese shop

shop

s3 > apothecary tinctura
s8 > elizabeth lindsay
creations
s13 > max
s20 > one home
s21 > oster jewelers
s22 > outdoor divas
s36 > the alchemist

note: all maps face north

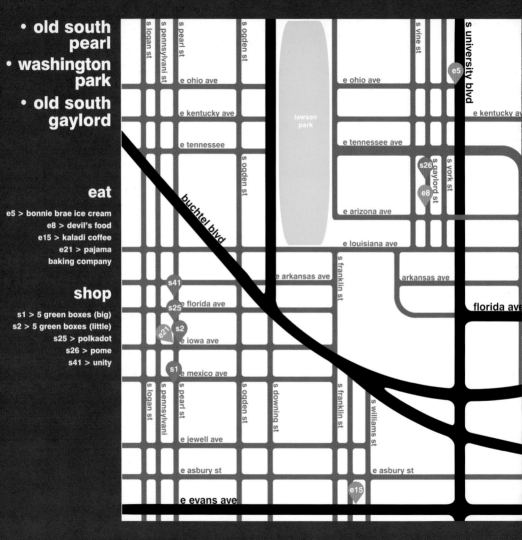

- **old south pearl**
- **washington park**
- **old south gaylord**

eat

e5 > bonnie brae ice cream
e8 > devil's food
e15 > kaladi coffee
e21 > pajama baking company

shop

s1 > 5 green boxes (big)
s2 > 5 green boxes (little)
s25 > polkadot
s26 > pome
s41 > unity

note: all maps face no

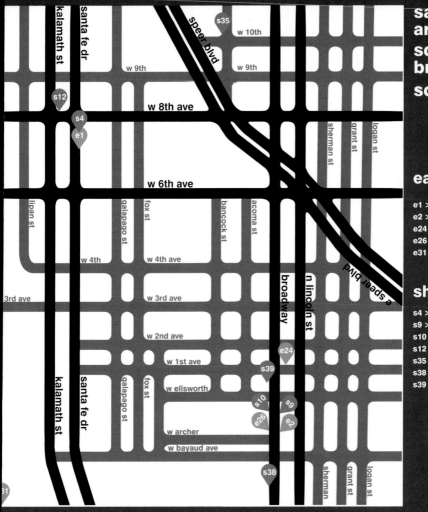

santa fe •
arts district
south •
broadway
southwest •

eat

e1 > arada
e2 > beatrice & woodsley
e24 > senor burrito
e26 > sputnik
e31 > tacos y salsas #3

shop

s4 > carol mier fashion
s9 > fancy tiger clothing
s10 > fancy tiger crafts
s12 > icelantic boards
s35 > the 400
s38 > thrifty sticks
s39 > true love

te: all maps face north

5 green boxes (big store)

the "home and lifestyle" store with items culled from around the world

1705 south pearl street. corner of mexico
303.282.5481 www.5greenboxes.com
winter mon - sat 10a - 6p sun noon - 5p
summer sun 9a - 5p

opened in 2004. owners: charlotte elich and carrie vadas
all major credit cards accepted
custom orders / design

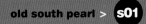

old south pearl > s01

"Home and lifestyle" doesn't quite capture the essence of the bigger of the two *5 Green Boxes* stores. It's more of an inspiration store. A dazzle-your-eyes-with-the-colors, the inventiveness, the tableaux, store. From their own custom production of distressed and felted furniture, to the hand-sewn kids' plush toys, the folks here have a knack not just for choosing great things, but for displaying them with distinctive flair and imagination. You will more than likely need five big boxes to take all of your new purchases out of here.

covet:
green box construction:
  boiled wool custom furniture
  painted rescued furniture
rise up t's
creative co-op mercury glass votives
mariachi imports recycled plastic rugs
dash & albert striped ticking totes
hand-picked guatemalan textiles

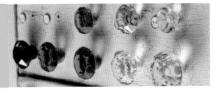

101

5 green boxes (little store)

the "body and ego" store

1596 south pearl street. corner of iowa
303.777.2331 www.5greenboxes.com
winter mon - sat 10a - 6p sun noon - 5p
summer mon - sat 10a - 6p sun 9a - 5p

opened in 1999. owners: charlotte elich and carrie vadas
all major credit cards accepted

old south pearl > 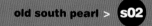 **s02**

Situated on a bright corner, the smaller *5 Green Boxes* sibling is a little jewel of a boutique. Walking in for the first time, I swelled with that happy sense that I would leave with something. I didn't know what, not even what category—which is what makes a store like this so much fun. Would it be a new linen baby-doll dress? Would it be killer indian-influenced slip-ons? A bag? A notebook? Earrings? Whatever the purchase, I knew I'd be fielding one question for a long time after my purchase: "where'd you get that?"

covet:
trinity cotton print dresses
matchpoint linen wear
maruca brocade bags
zents scents
bluefish sandals
raj slip-ons

apothecary tinctura

organic herbs and aromatherapy

2900 east sixth avenue. corner of fillmore
303.399.1175 www.apothecarytinctura.com
mon - fri 10a - 6p sat 10a - 5p sun noon - 4p

opened in 1997. owner: shelley torgove
all major credit cards accepted
classes. custom orders. consultations and body work

cherry creek north > s03

Apothecary Tinctura is my happy place. Descriptions that might work here include centering, calming, rejuvenating, soothing and empowering. There are scores of organic herbs here, from which you can blend teas, tinctures, poultices and brews. Then there's a variety of essential oils, incenses, natural body toiletries and enlightened baby products. But the soul of this store is the staff and their mission to promote health, well-being, and holistic care, especially to women, through workshops and their spa. Don't tell my editor, but I had a massage on my last day in town, and it was transformative.

covet:
apothecary tinctura essential herbs
big dipper beeswax candles
la luz angelica milk bath
rockin' baby slings
little twig baby products
pangea organics soaps
pure encapsulations
de vries hand-sourced chocolate

carol mier fashion

wearable and unique handcrafted clothes

754 santa fe drive. between 7th and 8th
303.446.0117 www.carolmierfashion.com
thu - sat by appointment first and third fri 6 - 9p

opened in 1992. owner: carol mier
all major credit cards accepted
custom orders / design. wardrobe consultations

santa fe arts district > **s04**

Carol Mier makes wearable art, which is appropriate as her store / atelier is smack-dab in the middle of the arts district. I came in when I saw her through the window, a lean silhouette in an asian-influenced patchwork coat and the most perfect velvety pants that fit tight through the thigh and opened into a dramatic bellbottom. Drama is definitely a factor in the clothes here although unlike most dramatic clothes, these actually are wearable, comfortable and even washable. Seems to me if you want to make a statement without a lot of hassle, Carol has the right pieces to add flair to your closet.

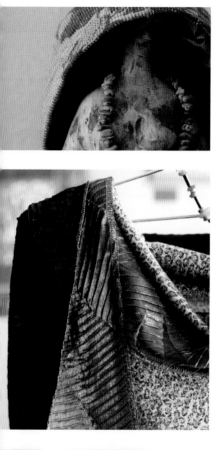

covet:
carol mier:
  long raw silk swing coat
  tulip skirt
  cocoon coat
  tapestry jacket
marc mccall earrings
holly fillingham jewelry
leyna bencomo jewelry

composition

still no tagline since 1993

7180 west alaska drive. between teller and saulsbury
303.894.0025 www.shopcomposition.com
mon - sat 10a - 7p sun 11a - 5p

opened in 1993. owner: jennifer roberts
all major credit cards accepted
online shopping

belmar >

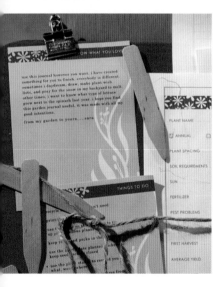

This book's cover may trumpet eat and shop, but the subtext to this series is design, design, design! At *Composition*, the *eat.shop guides* would feel right at home. There's an array of snappy products each bearing the unmistakable mark of being well-designed. Better still is the book section, with titles that analyze, exhibit, praise and generally promote the well-trained eye. This is a store for which you should block out a period of time—say 2 hours—and an amount of cash—you decide the number (in my case, a large number)—and nourish your design hunger.

covet:
rex ray notecards
ambrose/harris basics design books
imbibe magazine
escama metallic bags
unison bed linens
blue dot bed
offi pine lap table
orla kiely pocket shopper

cry baby ranch

cowboy furniture, cowgirl gifts and cowkid clothing

1421 larimer street. between 14th and 15th
303.623.3979 www.crybabyranch.com
mon - fri 10a - 7p sat 10a - 6p sun noon - 5p

opened in 1989. owner: roxanne thurman
all major credit cards accepted
online shopping

larimer square > 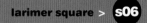 **s06**

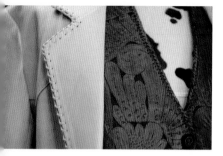

In less talented hands, *Cry Baby Ranch* might have become a campy outlet fueling America's craving for its Western mythos. Rather, owner Roxanne has created a brilliant store of singular focus. Everything in this brightly painted, well-stocked boutique—from the Hank Williams cutting board to the custom-upholstered vintage serape furniture pieces—speaks of the Wild West and its trappings. The apparel, jewelry and boots are all especially high caliber and unusual. If you're looking for the good, the bad and the unique—get here at high noon. You'll be unforgiven if you don't.

covet:
liberty handmade boots
sydney wydney mosaic vases
wyd & wox antique serape furniture
susan skinner reclaimed silver jewelry
margaret sullivan western jewelry
comstock heritage belt buckles
scully western coat jackets
kids' western books, toys & more

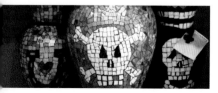

dragonfly

apparel for body and sole

3621 west 32nd avenue. between meade and lowell
303.433.6331 www.dragonflydenver.com
mon - sat 10a - 6p sun 11a - 4p

opened in 2003. owner: veronica hlatky
all major credit cards accepted
online shopping

highlands square > 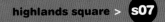 s07

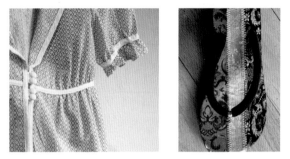

In one four day span while I was working on this book, the first day was 80°, the next day it snowed, the next day it was in the 70s and the next day it rained. Personally, I love varied weather, but it makes dressing challenging. The secret is layering, so a visit to *Dragonfly* would be helpful. With lots of flirty sweaters and skirts to choose from, you could layer up, then do your dance of the seven veils when the temperature shoots up again. I was one rainy day away from convincing myself I needed to buy a swingy silver coat here to complete my layered look. Then the sun came out and stayed. Damn.

covet:
seychelles platforms
trina turk silver coat
james jeans
porridge print shirts
muchacha chica chic
r jean jersey dress
ollie sang screen print t's
eva franco polka dot sweater

elizabeth lindsay creations

jewelry and gifties

3033 east third avenue. between milwaukie and saint paul
303.333.9989 www.elizabethlindsay.com
mon - fri 10a - 5:30p sat 10a - 5p

opened in 2008. owner: elizabeth lindsay
all major credit cards accepted
online shopping. custom orders / design

cherry creek north > **s08**

There's really only so much real estate on the human body on which to declare your allegiance to a cause, a person, a belief. After you've put on your business's baseball cap, your Greenpeace t-shirt and your Live Strong bracelet, there are not many more prominent places where you can make your statement. *Elizabeth Lindsay* has done us all a service with her token tags. These lightweight, silver and gold hand-stamped charms allow a wearer to mix, match and indefinitely add on to necklaces or bracelets. For about $25 bucks a pop, you can proclaim lots of causes. Hell, at that price you can contradict yourself.

covet:
hand-stamped silver & gold tags
essential stuff candles & soaps
oovoo hand-embroidered purses & bags
dani line shea & soy body butter
nomad skull & roses rainboots
zulugrass beaded grass necklaces
marybelle indonesian wrap skirts

fancy tiger clothing

clothes, bags and jewelry with panache for both women and men

14 south broadway. between ellsworth and bayaud
303.282.6590 www.fancytiger.com
mon - sat 11a - 7p sun noon - 6p

opened in 2008. owners: matthew brown and jaime jennings
mc. visa
custom orders. design

south broadway >  **s09**

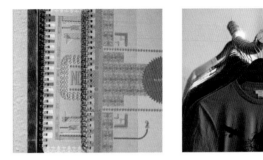

Matthew, co-owner of *Fancy Tiger Clothing*, is a cool cat. Not only is he Mr. Scoop with regard to happenings in town, but he also has insightful thoughts about retail trends, all the while speaking in glowing terms about his wife and co-owner Jaime. And wait, he also has great fashion sense, not just personally but in the selection sold at *Fancy Tiger*. But what really floored me was when he casually mentioned that he sews and produces a number of the bags and purses sold in the store. What? When? How? *Really?!* When does this man sleep?

> *covet:*
> pant & shorts created by matthew
> funklectic jewelry
> sam spitzer junk heart
> shel's crafty lockets
> it denim
> fluffyco screen-print t's
> fit printed bags
> brown sound striped sweaters

fancy tiger crafts

learn it, make it, wear it, love it
1 south broadway. corner of ellsworth
303.733.3855 www.fancytiger.com
mon - sat 11a - 7p sun noon - 6p tue 11a - 9p

opened in 2006. owners: amber corcoran and jaime jennings
mc. visa
online shopping. classes

south broadway > 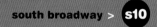 s10

For the past few years, knitting has been sweeping the nation. Magazines devoted to various sewing and soft crafts have multiplied like, well, patches on a crazy quilt. At *Fancy Tiger Crafts*, they've been abreast of the movement, if not ahead of it, since opening. While others are tackling their first rectangular scarf, the driven girls here are now on to spinning their own wools. With supplies galore, craft nights for learning and practicing, and a fun assortment of materials from Japan and beyond, go in ready to get hooked. You'll see how much you needed this in your life, knit-purl, knit-purl.

covet:
nature's palette yarns
amy butler fabrics
japanese craft supplies
lampe's lumps yarns
f-t felting kits
vintage fabrics
soft goods books & magazines
spinning supplies

gimme gimme pillow toast

asian pop goods for all

445 south saulsbury street. belmar block seven. between west virginia and alaska
303. 872.7706 www.gimmegimmepillowtoast.com
wed - sun noon - 7p

opened in 2006. owners: andrew novick and janene hurst
all major credit cards accepted
custom orders. gallery

belmar > **s11**

Everything Cute, Pop and Pink!!

A visit to *Gimme Gimme Pillow Toast* could spark a lot of academic graduate-level reflection about globalism, irony and the post-kawaii culture. Or it could, as it did to me, reveal how many flavors of Pocky there are that I didn't know about. True tastemakers, owners Andrew and Janene, have stocked their store with a number of marvels, most hand picked on their Asian travels. That impossible-to-shop-for brother will no doubt enjoy the rare gugu t-shirt you get him here. For your equally-hard-to-shop for sister, may I recommend the men's flavor Pocky?

covet:
dakin dream pets
wire robots
dydo american coffee
animal molds
pop ink napkins
gugu t's
nook art card holders
local art & photography

icelantic boards

948 west eighth avenue. between santa fe and kalamath
303.670.6804 www.icelanticboards.com
tue - fri 11a - 6p sat - mon by appointment only

opened in 2004. owner: ben anderson
all major credit cards accepted
custom designs

santa fe arts district > **s12**

I stumbled into *Icelantic Boards & Gallery* following a First Friday event, and found nobody home. Well, the shop dog was there, but otherwise, it was me and a roomful of strikingly artistic skis. And a keg. Trust me when I say this was a really effective way to get to know their range of in-house designed, Colorado-made, innovative skis. When I left, some time later (I finally figured out that I wandered in on a "by appointment only day. Duh.) I was certain that I wanted to feature this place helmed by a gang of passionate, homegrown skiers. These guys are real Colorado originals.

covet:
icelantic custom designed skis featuring iconic figures:
    scout
    pilgrim
icelantic:
  giraffe long-sleeve tee
  topsheet graphic reprints
  migration hat

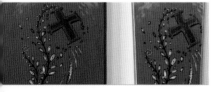

max

making a difference for women

3039 east third avenue. corner of saint paul
303.321.4949 www.maxfashion.com
mon - sat 10a - 6p sun noon - 5p

opened in 1985. onwer: max martinez
all major credit cards accepted

cherry creek north > **s13**

Walking into *Max* on a Friday night was my platonic ideal of shopping. All the salespeople were kitted out impeccably, demonstrating how sharp the chic merchandise can look. The eponymous Max was there and exceedingly friendly. The clothes were at turns glamorous and playful, and the shoes were banging. All this, and then I was offered a glass of wine. That part's not necessarily standard operating procedure, but this particular evening found most of Cherry Creek North's merchants in happy-hour mode. For insight into the Denver fashion scene and its charm, it's hard to beat *Max*.

covet:
bottega veneta stretch silk sheath
rick owens anything
pringle of scotland pop art shift
lainey diaphanous cashmere sweater
lanvin crinkle silver sandals
stella mccartney linen platforms
henry beguelin bags
beth orduna jewelry

125

max & me

women and children first
3867 tennyson street. corner of 38th
303.455.9663
mon noon - 5p tue - thu 11a - 6:30p fri 11a - 5p sat 10a - 5p sun 10a - 3p

opened in 2005. owner: anne thibert
mc. visa

highlands >  **s14**

At *Max & Me*, I achieved a real maternal milestone. For the first time since having my daughter eight years ago, I walked into a boutique, bypassed the kids' clothes, and began checking out all the great jeans. Almost a decade now, I've been magnetically drawn to the tiny shoes, onesies and baby hats first, and then if time allowed, I'd look for myself. But here, even though the kids' lines are absurdly cute, I found the pull of the jeans even stronger. So it's progress. Even though moms are trained to put kids first, this place helped me to momentarily put myself first—into new jeans, that is.

covet:
kasil jeans
signorelli t's
tag jeans
cat studio glasses
bishop pants
pebbles baby clothes
wallcandy arts
bobux kid shoes

metroboom

a stylin' revolution for men

1550 platte street, suite a/b. between 15th and 17th
303.477.9700 www.metroboom.com
tue - sat 10a - 7p

opened in 2005. owner: jung park
mc. visa
classes. custom orders. salon

lohi > **s15**

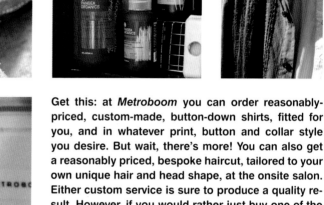

Get this: at *Metroboom* you can order reasonably-priced, custom-made, button-down shirts, fitted for you, and in whatever print, button and collar style you desire. But wait, there's more! You can also get a reasonably priced, bespoke haircut, tailored to your own unique hair and head shape, at the onsite salon. Either custom service is sure to produce a quality result. However, if you would rather just buy one of the fashion-forward items off the rack, you can do that too. For the clothes, that is. A haircut off the rack, at any price, is generally a bad idea, i.e. Donald Trump.

covet:
metroboom custom-tailored shirts
rifle denim
uomo venetto handcrafted silk ties
robert wayne shoes
don't tread on me shirts
bumpy pitch t's
pangea body products

mike's toys and hobbies

keeping it real for kids

3845 tennyson street. between utica and tennyson
303.455.2087
mon - sun noon - 8p

opened in 2006. owner: mike iroc
all major credit cards accepted
online shopping. classes

highlands > s16

I don't know what goes on in my young son Johnny's head when his birthday rolls around. He probably wants a WII, a portable dvd player and an ATV. But here's what I'm eyeing for this and all future birthdays: balsa wood planes, volcano science kits, diy boat kits and—I don't know—rocks and sticks. With the exception of the last two things, which we stock in our backyard, all the other items are available at *Mike's Toys and Hobbies*, which means that until Johnny moves out, I can happily shop at this fine store.

covet:
1/64 die-cast models
slot cars
constructo junior boat kits
estes rockets
model helicopters
testers enamels & lacquer
smithsonian science kits
kites

mod livin'

the intersection of timeless design and today's lifestyle
5327 east colfax avenue. between colorado and monaco
720.941.9292 www.modlivin.com
mon - sat 10a - 5:30p sun noon - 5p

opened in 2001. owners: erick and jill roorda
all major credit cards accepted
online shopping. registries. classes. custom orders / design

park hill > **s17**

A squad can be mod. Video games can be mod. But when your livin' is mod, that's as good as it gets. *Mod Livin'*, as defined by the gang on East Colfax, includes outfitting your home with some timeless retro pieces, like a Brown & Saltman buffet; some modern irony, like a Harry Allen chrome piggy bank; then adding in some sweet, locally designed steel cabinetry for a genuinely modern, as in current, touch. The whole effect, as you see in this multi-room tribute to the best of the old and new together, is stylin'.

covet:
steve bennett @ housefish
 powder-coated steel cabinetry
verpan ball light
harry allen chrome pig
italian glass liquor set
brown & saltman cabinet
holly aiken vinyl bags
fresco baby chair

mona lucero

devotion to style

2544 15th street. between boulder and central
303.458.0090 www.monalucero.com
mon - tue 2 - 6:30p wed - sat noon - 6:30p sun noon - 3p

opened in 2002. owner: mona lucero
all major credit cards accepted
online shopping. custom orders. gallery

lohi > **s18**

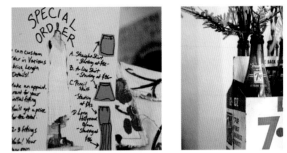

Mona lists as her inspirations Moschino, Miyake, Vreeland and Schiaparelli—a bunch of iconoclasts if ever there were. No surprise then to find that Mona has taken an icon as familiar as the yellow smiley face and subverted it into a familiar but funny, fuzzy t-shirt. Her background in both art and fashion manifests in all her designs, and nowhere is it more evident than in her killer concept drawings. Who knows what percentage of her designs get off the board, but I'd like to officially declare my interest in the fur overalls with vinyl belt I saw sketched out. Moschino would approve, I think.

covet:
mona lucero:
  cotton twill kimono jacket
  fuzzy smiley t's
goorin bros. hats
kali kali puckered t's
pearl embellished sweater
elzwear men's screened t's
blue q messenger bags

moss pink

flora and botanical

4615 east 23rd avenue. between dexter and cherry
303.388.1666 www.mosspinkflora.com
mon - fri 9a - 6p sat 10a - 5p

opened in 2006. owner: jil schlisner
all major credit cards accepted
online shopping. gift baskets. classes. custom orders

park hill > **s19**

First, credit must go to Jil for the name of her flower and gift store. *Moss Pink* is a wonderfully evocative name, even if you've never seen the lush carpets of little pink flowers that bloom in spring. I was lured in by the name but stayed for the gorgeous floral arrangements being shaped right in the middle of the store. Watching bouquets take form in the perfumed air can be a little hypnotic, and I admit to some reluctance to leave. Nice then, that you can take some of the spirit of the store home with you with the winsome gift and houseware items sold there.

covet:

gorgeous floral arrangements
parasol hummingbird feeders
venetian vase
middle kingdom chinese pottery vases
design ideas lamella vase
mercury glass perfume bottles
voluspa body products

one home

modern, contemporary furniture and design services
2445 east third avenue. corner of columbine
720.946.1505 www.onehomedesign.com
mon - fri 10a - 6p sat 10a - 4p

opened in 2002. owner: heather mourer
all major credit cards accepted
custom orders / design

cherry creek north > 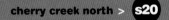 s20

There are those out there with second homes or, heavens, multiple homes, but most of us have only one home, and we want to make sure it reflects our personality. If your personality is modern, classic, worldly, but appreciative of local resources, then your furnishings await at *One Home*, with design services available to boot. I was particularly smitten with the work of local fourth-generation woodworker Ethan Hutchinson and his carved and curvy black walnut occasional chair. This is exactly the kind of piece I desire for my one home.

covet:
double butter wood buffet
bonacina wicker egg chair
ethan hutchinson curved chair
mike mcclung burnt vellum mixed media
jack middleton sculpture
mccoy collage side table
sundial clock sculpture
fritz hansen swan & egg chairs

oster jewelers

a watch and jewelry boutique

251 steele street. between second and third
303.572.1111 www.osterjewelers.com
tue - fri 10:30a - 6p sat 10:30a - 5:30p

opened in 2003. owners: melissa and jeremy oster
all major credit cards accepted
online shopping. classes. custom orders / design

cherry creek north > 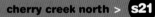 **s21**

Our dog Joya goes to work with my husband Abe every day and was awarded for her diligence with a plastic nameplate to velcro onto Abe's cubicle. Mojo goes to work with her owners Jeremy and Melissa, the proprietors of *Oster Jewelers,* and is honored with a Santagostino ring, chockablock with precious and semi-precious stones and enameled charms. Yowza. It pays to have owners with flair and connections. The Osters have both and have made their store into a haven for jewelry enthusiasts seeking unusual, commissioned or just downright gorgeous adornments. Joya is jealous.

covet:

arman diamond iron cross necklace
oster pearls
giuliano mazzuoli manometro watches
u-boat big face watches
sevan mixed stone 24 karat quartz ring
arunashi gold link chain
alex soldier sunflower ring
ulysse nardin watches

outdoor divas

women are not small men

2717 east third avenue. between detroit and clayton
303.320.3482 www.outdoordivas.com
mon - sat 10a - 6p sun 11a - 5p

opened in 2006. owners: mike callus and kim walker
all major credit cards accepted
online shopping. classes

cherry creek north > **s22**

No, women are not small men, as the tagline to *Outdoor Divas* attests. Some women, ahem, are bigger. So the tagline doesn't necessarily apply to me, but I get the meaning. Women want to have all the outdoor fun, in surf, snow and sun, and look stylish doing it. Or, perhaps like me, some want to have all the stylish gear but not actually do that outdoorsy stuff. I figure the owners won't object to me purchasing a yoga skirt, which will never see a downward dog but will see a few go down the hatch. So whether you're a genuine outdoor diva or just playing the part, here's the place to suit up.

covet:
patagonia
k2
burton
brooks
prana
kjus
volkl

pandora jewelry

jewelry, glasses and fun stuff

220 east 13th avenue. between grant and sherman
303.832.7073 www.pandorajewelrydenver.com
mon - sat 10a - 7p sun 11a - 5p

opened in 1993. owners: stephanie shearer, chris bacorn and carol tervo
all major credit cards accepted
online shopping. registries. gift baskets. custom orders

capitol hill >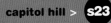

The Pandora of Greek mythology opened the original can of whoop-ass onto the world, releasing envy, greed and vanity, among other evils. This was problematic for a number of reasons. If vanity didn't exist, would I really need Megan Kelley's retro jewelry? If greed didn't exist, could I survive without that unbelievably covetable Japanese owl tea set? If envy weren't a factor, would I have given the stink-eye to the woman who *did* buy the owl tea set while I was there? No, we can't blame *Pandora Jewelry* for all these emotions, but they do certainly seem present here.

covet:
kotobuki owl tea set
paper blanks dayplanner
day of the dead hand-picked items
jessica jeanne pillowcase totes
megan kelley jewelry
hb glass design rings
harriet's little soap company
la vie parisienne earrings

plastic chapel

designer toys with cult followings

3109 east colfax avenue. corner of saint paul
303. 722. 0715 www.plasticchapel.com
tue - sun noon - 6p

opened in 2005. owners: deanna webb and david wendt
all major credit cards accepted
online shopping. gallery

city park >  **s24**

Oddly, *Plastic Chapel* gave me my first missionary experience. I brought from here a handful of blind-box zippits zipper pulls for my children to share with their friends. None had ever had zipper pulls before—they'd never even heard of them. When I introduced the pulls, they then realized their previous life had been a sham and they now needed zipper pulls to be complete. So be forewarned when you enter this chapel of plastic and find the dozens of designer toy lines you didn't know existed. You too will have to reexamine the life you've lived without the goods from here.

covet:
mike graves designer toys
super rad axis of evil figurines
exclusive unkl unipo series
kidrobot me i'm french dunny series
cardboy robots
hazmate plush toys
teenpops plush aliens
strangeco oink le rouge

polkadot

get your dot on

1577 south pearl street. between florida and iowa
303.282.4307 www.polkadotdenver.com
tue - sat 11a - 6p sun noon - 4p

opened in 2005. owner: dezi gellman
all major credit cards accepted
custom orders

old south pearl > 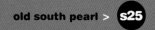 **s25**

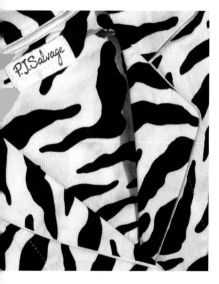

Polkadot owner Dezi urges you to get your dot on, a directive that is open to interpretation. Take it literally, and you might find yourself wearing some perennially popular (and perpetually cute) polkadotted clothes and accessories. Think of it in broader terms, and it might mean to get a little "dotty" and purchase some of the kooky and fun gift items she carries, like the silver fortune cookies. Maybe you want to dot some Thymes lotion onto your thirsting skin? Or get exotic and slide into some wild zebra-striped pyjamas. Whatever your dotting pleasure, you can find it here.

covet:
dezi bags
p.j. salvage pajamas
julia mcclure dog paintings
jennywear jewelry
bella sera baby bib
happy green bee
lulu bella paintings
crystal sharp jewelry

149

pome

not shabby chic, sweety chic
1018 south gaylord street. between mississippi and tennessee
303.722.2900 www.pomedenver.com
tue - sat 10a - 5p sun 11a - 3p

opened in 2005. owner: kate feinsod
all major credit cards accepted
gift baskets. custom orders

old south gaylord > s26

An apple is a pome. So is a pear and a quince. The name, it turns out, refers to a kind of flowering fruit. So *Pome's* owner, Kate, named her shop to convey a place where artists could flower. In the varied offerings at *Pome,* you see the work of many artists from different disciplines, including fine art, textiles and crafts. Some have likened the *Pome* aesthetic to Shabby Chic, but I like it way more than that. It has a certain vintage appeal that celebrates people experimenting while not losing touch with old-fashioned themes. There are more than a few good apples here.

covet:
golden pear vintage children's clothing
margo belle headbands
seda france candles
chandler collection linens
jil capuccio boy's intage-inspired bowling shirt
european soaps
vintage letterpress cards
sam robinson bride-to-be-kit

red door swingin'

a mélange of home and gift items

2556 fifteenth street. corner of umatilla
303.433.6900 www.reddoorswingin.com
see website for hours

opened in 2003. owner: suzanne blaylock
mc. visa
online shopping

lohi >

I ducked into *Red Door Swingin'* on a rainy day when everything appeared gloomy. Even the vintage bike parked out front, with its cheerful bouquet of flowers, seemed unusually morose. But inside here, everything was perky. The tables were draped in bright linens, the lights broke through the grayness, and fluorescent feathers peeked out from glassware and candle displays. It was hard for me to bid adieu to this spirit-lifting refuge, but I had my appointed rounds. May I recommend *Red Door Swingin'* as a superior alternative to an umbrella?

covet:
matt n nat vegan handbags
seascape lampshades
goosetown distressed revived furniture
scheme candles
french bull robot plates
dovetail pottery
built laptop cases

rejuvanest

gifts, décor and furnishings for you and your nest
3719 west 32nd avenue. corner of meade
303.455.1504
tue - fri 11a - 6p sat 10a - 7p sun 11a - 4p

opened in 2007. owner: brenda meyers
mc. visa
online shopping. registries. gift baskets. custom orders

highlands square > 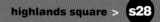

It took me a while to link the nest in this store's name to owner Brenda's appreciation for birds and their home environments. A perching sparrow here, a tiny miniature nest there, until I finally clued in to the understated theme at *Rejuvanest*. My inner magpie began to chirp as I envisioned all these lovely things coming home and shining up my own nest. Each room of this converted 19th-century house glitters with objects that will add warmth, style and fun. Pajamas in the bedroom, kids' clothes in the nursery, bath and beauty items in the bathroom. Time to get featherin'.

covet:
jeremie faux bois plate set
tag stitched table linens
roost vase & perching sparrow
bela bum bum lingerie
sweet pea jewelry
kara rosenberry vintage photo cards
italian hanging flower ceramics
archipelago soy candles

rockmount ranch wear

the reference point for real western wear
1626 wazee street. between 16th and 17th
303.629.7777 www.rockmount.com
mon - fri 7a - 5p sat 11a - 5p sun 11a - 4p

opened in 1946. owner: jack a. weil
all major credit cards accepted
online shopping. custom orders / design

lodo > **s29**

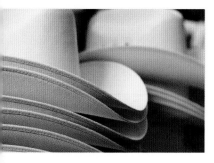

Rockmount is legendary. It brought us the western snap pocket, without which presumably there could be no emo. It outfitted both Jake and Heath in B*rokeback Mountain*, which may explain why their characters couldn't quit each other. Ronald Reagan wore *Rockmount*. The eclectic list goes on, demonstrating the line's universal appeal. Captained by the "world's oldest CEO," 107-year-old "Papa" Jack A. Weil, *Rockmount* has been making crowd-pleasing Western clothing and accessories for more than 60 years. Whether young or old, blue stater or red stater, you'll love *Rockmount*.

covet:
embroidered snap western shirts
chamois riding skirts
original silk artist commissioned ties
fur, wool, felt, straw & raffia hats
suede shirts
leather jackets & fringe jackets
western memorabilia

sportique scooters

where scooters come from

3211 pecos street. corner of 32nd
303.477.8614 www.sportiquescooters.com
tue - fri 10a - 7p sat 10a - 5p
see website for additional locations

opened in 1998. owners: adam baker and colin shattuck
all major credit cards accepted
online shopping. rallies. custom orders

highlands >  s30

Now I get it. Three years ago, writing about a scooter store back East, I didn't get it. Gas savings, shmash savings, I'll take mine supersized, please. Cut to today—to global warming, sky-high prices at the pump, to green everything. Now, I want a scooter. I need a scooter. I called my husband from *Sportique* and told him to have a scooter waiting for me when I got home, so aroused was I by the fine selection and lifestyle promoted at this store. It's not just the scooters, though, you know. The '60s-era scooter dress has come back too. I'm a convert now. Viva la vespa!

covet:
scooters:
  genuine, buddy, kimeo, sym, aprilia & vespa
corazzo jackets
chrome bags
helmet city helmets
guardian seat covers
vintage service & restoration

strut

shoes, handbags and accessories with style

3611 west 32nd avenue. near lowell
303.477.3361 www.strutdenver.com
mon - thu 11a - 6p fri 11a - 5p sat 10a - 5p sun 11a - 4p

opened in 2005. owner: elyse burja
all major credit cards accepted
online shopping

highlands >  s31

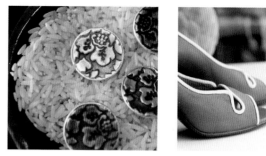

There are probably carriage lessons offered at your local finishing school that will teach you to walk with grace and confidence. Or, you could slip on sizzling metallic gold Blay heels and set the pavement afire. Nothing ratchets up my sauciness like a great pair of shoes. Just entering the perfectly named *Strut* added BTU's to my normal sense of self. Watch out then, when I walk out of this impressive store. I'll be the one sashaying a wide path, with sparks coming off my Chie Mahara pumps.

covet:
biviel silver sandals
blay gold heels
tsubo flats
chie mahara spectator pumps
tpu sole pumps
brave leather & silver bracelets
slainte bags

studio bead

jewelry, beading supplies and events
3716 west 32nd avenue. corner of meade
303.777.1813 www.studiobead.com
tue - sat 11a - 6:30p sun 10a - 4p

opened in 2005. owner: joy barrett
mc. visa
classes. custom orders / design

highlands square > **s32**

For all you Frida Kahlo lovers out there, and you know who you are (hint: you've penciled in the mono-brow on occasion when nobody was looking), you need to mark your calendar for the annual Beads, Braids & Brow event at *Studio Bead*, typically scheduled around Frida's birthday in July. You can purchase Frida-themed gifts or channel her artistic energies into your own beading art. If that's not a good time to visit because you're off with your muralist paramour, say, come any other day and take in the jewelry, gift items, and yes, beads, that make this store so fun.

covet:
dtown designs trinket necklaces
pearl reconstructed skirts & shirts
bead of the heart gems
fridastyle jewelry
cre-asian origami earrings
looking glass beads

swank

high fashion on an approachable scale
2405 west 32nd avenue. corner of zuni
303.433.6116 www.swankdenver.com
tue - fri 11a - 6p sat 11a - 5p

opened in 2005. owner: wendy van der maas
all major credit cards accepted
online shopping

highlands >  **s33**

Power, passion and fashion are all that *Swank* promises. I'll take two of each, please. Owner Wendy has built a store that seems like a brick-and-mortar version of herself—long and slender and graced with great clothes. I coveted a teal dress with an asymmetrical neckline in a fine jersey material that you probably have to be long and slender to get away with wearing. But it's ok because unlike so many boutiques, *Swank* doesn't discriminate against those of us with curves (and muffintops). Power, passion and fashion for all is only a visit away.

covet:
kitchen orange asymmetrical dress
nu collective empire waist dress
luna rosa jewelry
william rast denim
hudson denim
ollie sang tapestry jackets
get fresh body products
wendy way paintings

talulah jones

your home. your kid. you.

1122 east 17th avenue. between downing and park
303.832.1230 www.talulahonline.com
mon - fri 10a - 6p sat 10a - 5p sun 11a - 4p

opened in 2001. owner: robin lohre
mc. visa
online shopping. registries. custom orders / design

uptown >

I'm a fool for the name Talulah and have pledged that I will visit anyplace that features Talulah in its name. I would shop at *Talulah's Parachute Pants Emporium* or eat at *Talulah's Rancid Cabbage Grille* if either existed. I'm awfully grateful though that *Talulah Jones* is an exquisite, whimsical, happy place that doesn't test my resolve for these kinds of bizarre personal dares. It's a light-filled store that specializes in quaint, cute and fun items for your home, your kid and you. Or, as somebody poetically said, it's where you find the things that make your house a home.

covet:
christy lea payne jewelry
lizzie keinast paintings
rachel nathan prints
jellycat plush animals
la vie necklaces & bracelets
kathi kruse handmade dolls
marie belle teas
teaposy glass teapots

167

the 400

you make the statement, they provide the means
1010 bannock street. corner of 10th
303.446.0400 www.the400.net
mon - thu 10a - 6p fri 10a - 7p sat noon - 7 sun noon - 6p

opened in 2005. owners: randy kleiner and kris fry
mc. visa
phone shopping

southwest > 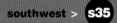 s35

In the gilded age, Mrs. William Astor invited 400 social elites to a ball at her mansion, and an exclusive though unofficial club, The 400, was conceived. You didn't lobby to get in; you were either in or you weren't. This spirit is maintained at Denver's high-end shoe store, *The 400*. A pair of limited-edition sneakers may go unnoticed by the world at large, but the other sneaker aficionados will know for sure. And boom, you're in the club. You can talk the talk all you want, but you don't count until you walk the walk, in the right shoes.

covet:
adidas consortium
nb super team
nike urban energy / indie
creative recreation
vans
the hundreds
a life
kidrobot

the alchemist

exclusive european toiletries, perfumes and cosmetics

2737 east third avenue. corner of detroit
303.377.7567
mon - sat 10a - 5:30p sun by chance

opened in 2007. owner: marisa a. medina
all major credit cards accepted
gift baskets. private parties

cherry creek north > s36

I find myself in the somewhat odd situation of being a bath-and-beauty-product consumer while not actually employing them all. I was only half joking when I coined "lather, rinse, repeat next week" for my motto. So the problem arises when I go to a thrilling store like *The Alchemist*, teeming with its floor-to-ceiling displays of products that set my heart aflutter. Vintage-inspired glass perfume bottles with mystical scents. Art nouveau scripts written in gilt lettering on magical cream jars. Fragrant soaps pressed into nature's shapes. I want to take them all home.

covet:
nuxe anti-wrinkle cream
mor fruits of cornucopia hand cream
jack black hair pomade
olivina bath soap
le petit prince kids' bath products
s. maria novella olio da bagno
thymes wild ginger mist
maximal art fleur de lis necklace

the fabric lab

3105 east colfax. between saint paul and milwaukee
303.321.3604 www.thefabriclab.com
wed - sat noon - 6p

opened in 2002. owners: josh and tran willis
visa. mc
custom orders/design

city park >  **s37**

The Fabric Lab has that anything-goes collective feel. You might arrive during a patron's haircut, a gallery exhibit or when the media (like me? No, like the New York Times) are trolling to find out what's the real deal in the Denver arts and culture scene. *The Fabric Lab* will tell you, "we keep it realer" and it would appear they do with their rotating schedule of happenings. Of course, they also sell pieces from local designers whose medium is often reconstructed vintage clothes—that's the fabric part of the name. And everything has the experimental feeling of trying new things—that's the lab.

covet:
love las muertas
potential fashion
denver magpie
purse fairy
shammy
craze one

thrifty stick

skater owned and operated since 1998

135 south broadway. corner of maple
303.282.8972 www.thriftystick.com
mon - sat 11a - 7p sun 11a - 5p

opened in 1998. owner: bryan dehaven
all major credit cards accepted
camps and lessons

south broadway >  s38

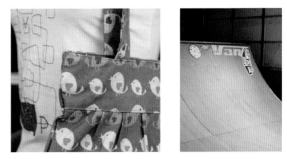

Denver has a robust skateboarding scene, with a city-supported downtown multi-bowl skatepark and a whole lot of unsanctioned action throughout the rest of the city. How excellent, then, that Denver has Colorado's only skateboarding museum. Granted, it's located in *Thrifty Stick*, a lifestylesque board-and-gear store, but this way you don't have to pay admission to check it out. And if I can give a bit of advice, the impressive display of boards from the '70s and '80s should influence your retro-skate look today.

covet:
volcam
element
obey
rvca
zoo york
innes
spitfire
vans

true love

playful shoes you can afford

42 broadway. corner of irvington
303.860.8783 www.trueloveshoes.com
mon - sun 11a - 7p

opened in 2006. owner: sarah lilly-ray
all major credit cards accepted

south broadway >  **s39**

Sarah, the owner of *True Love*, is not concerned with brand names. She's much more interested in her clientele's ability to buy a snazzy shoe and, then, as she puts it, "still have money left over for champagne." Frugality has its place (although apparently not around me) and I give props to Sarah for her concept of keeping shoes under $50. What I really appreciate, however, is her commitment to vegan shoes and accessories. Leopard-spotted, peek-a-boo toes can be pretty racy. Racier still when you can say, "no animals were harmed in the making of these hot pink stilettos."

covet:
classified
soda
delicious
miss me
melie bianco
redtoo

177

twist & shout

a must for music lovers

2508 east colfax avenue. corner of columbine
303.722.1943 www.twistandshout.com
mon - sat 10a - 10p sun 10a - 8p

opened in 1988. owner: paul and jill epstein
all major credit cards accepted
online shopping

city park >  **s40**

It's all part of my rock 'n' roll fantasy. It's all part of my rock 'n' roll dream. Honestly, *Twist & Shout* could be the setting for any of my more lurid fantasies which might include a tryst with Thom Yorke, in the sound-baffled dance and hip-hop glass-walled room while a Cocteau Twins remix drones on and the RCA dog looks on un-blinkingly. But twisted fantasies aside, *Twist & Shout* is a truly epic music store, with serious audiophiles on staff, a great and vast collection of rare music, books and dvds and an impressive gallery of local tour posters. This place should be fantasy enough for me.

covet:
vinyl:
  reissues
  imports
  small labels
rare posters
rock 'n' roll books
dvds
collectibles

unity

men and women can unite here

1455 south pearl street. between florida and arkansas
720.570.5076 www.unityboutique.com
mon - thu 11a - 6p fri - sat 11a - 7p sun noon - 5p

opened in 2007. sarah husslon and megan smith
all major credit cards accepted
online shopping

old south pearl > 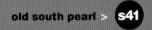 **s41**

My fave Denver clothing purchase came from *Unity*: a tissue thin, airbrushed, pleated and polka-dotted Oramami long t-shirt. Sounds ghastly when I describe it, but it's positively dazzling when on. There wasn't the question of if I would find something with such panache at *Unity*; it was a question of when. As it happened, my eyes alighted on the t-shirt after I already had my hands full with five or six other contenders. Now this shirt, which trumped all comers, is my absolute go-to when I need to look fresh. Make sure you check out *Unity* if you need to have one of those in your wardrobe.

covet:
super lucky cat recycled clothing
oramami tissue t's
same underneath organic cotton jackets
miel pink label dresses
denim of virtue jeans
melissa jelly shoes
isda white label dresses
commando underwear

urban lifestyle

home, gift and design goods
1720 wazee street, #1b. between 17th and 18th
303.572.7900 www.myurbanlifestyle.com
mon - sat 10:30a - 6p

opened in 2003. owners: steven whitney and mark lewis
all major credit cards accepted
online shopping. registries. custom orders / design

lodo >

Located in an area of town swelling with architects, *Urban Lifestyle* is essentially the gift shop annex to Architects Row. You'll find here not only the magazines and books that appeal to the design crowd, but certainly some of the European modern influenced housewares—tables, lamps, bedding and bric a brac (that's pronouced bree ah brah)—that you would probably find in the architects' actual homes. And if you fear this is only a place for design wonks, think again. There's whimsical items sprinkled throughout which keeps things light. Urban meets urbane here and it works beautifully.

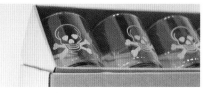

covet:
michael aram sona vessel
phaidon architectural books
iittala toikka little bird dinnerware
harry organizer
vy & elle splatter notebooks
magpie silver tableware
rios clementi hale studio city plates
daub & bauble lotions

wordshop.

invite. announce. scribe. send.

3180 meade street. corner of 32nd
303.477.9673 www.wordshopdenver.com
tue - sat 11a - 6p sun noon - 5p

opened in 2008. owner: jill alyn
visa. mc
custom orders / design

highlands square > 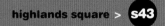 **s43**

revive the written word.

Here's where I wish poetry were the *eat.shop* métier. I would string together muscular lines extolling the virtues of a store that promotes all things epistolary —paper and pen, thank you notes and social letter-head, cards and journals, books about etiquette and tips on writing. In other words, words and their can-vases. Alas, though, I shall write as I do, in my usual prose. So gentle reader, believe me when I say, I love *Wordshop.*, and I entreat you to pay them a visit. I know you'll feel the same. Sincerely, Jan.

covet:
cards by
 lucky onion
 bumble ink
 giving
 jacki paper
 fresh frances
nantaka joy journals
writing, style & etiquette books

185

notes

notes

notes

etc.

the eat.shop guides were created by kaie wellman and are published by cabazon books

for more information about the series, or to buy print or online books, please visit: eatshopguides.com

eat.shop denver was written, researched and photographed by jan faust

editing: kaie wellman   copy editing: lynn king   fact checking: emily mattson
map and layout production: julia dickey

jan thx: i offer heartfelt thanks to angela berardino, the oxford hotel, all the wonderful people of denver, and most of all, to my navigator, johnny.

cabazon books: eat.shop denver
ISBN-13 978-0-9799557-2-3

copyright 2008 © cabazon books

every effort has been made to ensure the accuracy of the information in this book. however, certain details are subject to change. please remember when using the guides that hours alter seasonally and sometimes sadly, businesses close. the publisher cannot accept responsibility for any consequences arising from the use of this book.

the eat.shop guides are distributed by independent publishers group: www.ipgbook.com

PRINTED IN CHINA